Contents

Introduction

This booklet accompanies the four BBC programmes *Let's Write Poetry.* Learning objectives for the four programmes are based on the Performing Poetry and Creating Poetry strands in the primary strategy 'poetry progression' for years 5 and 6, found at www.standards.dfes.gov.uk:

Year 5:

- vary pitch, pace, volume, expression and use pauses to create impact
- use actions, sound effects, musical patterns, images and dramatic interpretation

- invent nonsense words and situations and experiment with unexpected word combinations
- use carefully observed details and apt images to bring subject matter alive; avoid cliché in own writing
- write free verse; use or invent repeating patterns; attempt different forms, including rhyme for humour

Year 6:

- vary pitch, pace volume, rhythm and expression in relation to the poem's meaning and form
- use actions, sound effects, musical patterns, images and dramatic interpretation, varying presentations by using ICT

- use language imaginatively to create surreal, surprising, amusing and inventive poetry
- use simple metaphors and personification to create poems based on real or imagined experience
- select pattern or form to match meaning and own voice

All four programmes follow a similar format. Sixteen children spend five days staying at Nethercourt Farm in Devon. The farm belongs to Michael and Clare Morpurgo and is one of the City Farms which children from city areas visit to experience country life.

The children are divided into four groups. On day one, each group is set a challenge – to write a polished poem during the week that will be performed on the final day. Each group is challenged to write a different sort of poetry. There is a resident poet at the farm to help the children. They visit the farm and look around the area and the house for inspiration. In each programme several poems are performed for the children. These too are used for inspiration and guidance, sometimes offering suggested approaches or formats for the children's own poetry.

During their stay, each group has a special visitor – a poet arrives to provide extra support and to read. The groups are provided with notebooks so that they can jot down and develop ideas. They also have cameras in order to photograph anything that might make a good stimulus. When writing they have dictionaries, thesauruses and rhyming dictionaries to help.

Using the pack

This pack consists of a DVD, four chapters of teacher's notes and PCMs of the poems used in the programmes, plus the four extra poems featured on the DVD. The teacher's notes for each programme follow the same format:

Writing warm up games gives ideas to practise skills and tune the children into a creative mood. These games can be played before or after the programme – or during it, if you wish to stop at various points.

Using the programme uses writing ideas that arise from the programme or from related ideas that work well

Using the poems shows how to use the poems in the programmes as models for the children's own poetry

Meet the poet gives background information on the poet featured in the programme

It is always helpful to write a class poem together so that the children have seen how to approach their writing. Brainstorming or listing ideas and words before writing is also helpful. Write up the basic toolkit: *choosing powerful words, observing details, using the senses, using alliteration, similes, metaphor, personification* and *your imagination*.

You may wish to use the poetry readings as a basis for comprehension but also as models for the children's own performances. Finally, it may be worth asking your class to discuss the quality of the children's poems read at the end of each programme. Which aspects are powerful and effective? Where might improvements be made? How well did they perform?

Poems used in the programmes

PROGRAMME 1 – OBSERVATION

Programme 1 focuses on the *detailed recreation of closely observed experience* strand outlined in the primary strategy 'poetry progression'. The programme is about learning to look carefully at the truth of an experience and how to use words to capture and preserve the essence of the experience. Ted Hughes wrote about this sort of writing in *Poetry in the Making* (Faber) and you may wish to read extracts from chapter one where he discusses how he wrote observation poems.

The challenge set in this programme is to: *write and perform a poem; written in free verse; based on a closely observed experience; describing details, using the senses.*

You will need some sort of focus for writing in your classroom – this could involve using a location nearby, bringing an object into the classroom or using photographs or video.

Writing warm up games

The following games are intended to help children generate words and ideas, to observe closely, use powerful language, similes and metaphor.

Warming up the mind

Start by playing a word association game – just to get the children generating words and ideas rapidly – a sort of linguistic mental gymnastics. You say a word and the children have one minute in which to jot down as many words as possible. Ideas that work well: *bonfire, snow, rough sea, night time, city centre, thunderstorm.* Then try the same thing using different objects or images. Now they are having to look and respond, generating words and ideas rapidly. Encourage them to look closely – as if they were a microscope – and to jot down words and phrases, thinking about what it looks like or reminds them of.

The point of this game is to begin to establish the idea of *brainstorming* – generating words and ideas to select from. If the children find it hard then begin with lots of whole-class brainstorming where you scribe their words and ideas onto a board. Keep this rapid and push them to generate as many words and ideas as possible.

Developing poetic technique

Using 'powerful' words Provide the children with sentences that are dull and use weak language, e.g. *The cat went along the wall.* Children have to spot the weak words and change them *(the Siamese crept along the wall).* They could also add in words *(The curious cat crept along the brick wall).* Make sure you discuss the dangers of 'overwriting' *(the one eared, down at heel, kind, shy, slim, slender, thin cat...),* and talk about the importance of making sure that if an adjective is used, it adds something powerful, new and necessary *(the shy giant* not *the big giant).* Aim for: powerful verbs *(crept* not *went);* necessary adjectives *(rusty letterbox* rather than *red letterbox);* precise nouns *(Siamese* rather than *cat);* and interesting details.

Inventing similes ('like' or 'as') This can be done by inventing wacky, exaggerated images, e.g. *as cross as a snarling wasp in a traffic jam, as slow as a snail stuck on superglue.* Ban the obvious clichés. So for *as thin as...,* I would not accept *pin, air, paper, stick, twig* etc. Encourage the children to seek something totally new, e.g. *as thin as a strand of hair from a tiger's tail.*

Try working from an object, image or something simple like a crescent moon – generate similes using 'like', e.g. *The moon is like an eyelash, a hump backed bridge, a clown's smile, a nursery rhyme boat.*

Using metaphors To introduce metaphors, invent new, true similes from close observation. Use objects or photos *(the bee's legs are like scaffold poles, its wings like a stained glass net).* Then demonstrate how to turn the similes into metaphors: *The bee's legs are like scaffold poles* could become *The bee's legs are scaffold poles.*

Or move the image to create the metaphor: *the bee's scaffold pole legs*. Explain that similes say that one thing is *like* another whereas metaphors say that one thing *is* another. Provide a list of similes and practice turning them into metaphors.

Personification Demonstrate how to bring an object alive as if it were a human or creature by using a verb, e.g. *the rain tiptoes*. It can help to have a picture of a scene. Make a list of things you can see, e.g. *lightning, thunder, clouds, rain, wind,* etc. Then make a list of verbs that are things that humans do, e.g. *whisper, dash, leap, giggle, dream,* etc. Then bring the verbs and nouns together, e.g. *lightning stabs the ground, thunder clears its throat, clouds dash by, rain stuns the streets, the wind whispers across the city...*, etc

Using sound effects Play a quick fire alliterative game. This could begin with you saying an animal – e.g. *dog* – and the children thinking of alliterative phrases or sentences – *a dirty dog dug a deep ditch deviously*.

Collect good examples Get the children collecting examples of alliteration, similes and metaphor, and inventing their own examples. Discuss their effect and write them up on a wall chart.

Using the programme

Writing a senses list poem

Generate a word bank together for the senses. Use headings for the each sense and then list ideas under each heading. What do you like to taste – what tastes do you not like? Turn their ideas into simple poetic sentences, e.g. *I want to taste the sharp tang of lemon, I want to taste the sizzle of bacon.*

Demonstrate how to write a more interesting 'senses' poem, by mixing the senses up, e.g. *I want to touch the scent of smoke lingering in the autumn air.*

Encourage interesting ideas and push the children to select words and ideas with care. Establish the notion that the first thought is not always the best thought – keep sifting and fishing for ideas and then select the most powerful. Let the children write their own senses list poem using their own ideas.

Writing about a focus

Help the children to select something to write about – and to look carefully for details, using their senses – jotting down words, ideas and similes. They could take photos of potential subjects. Writing on location can work well – find somewhere near the school: *a park, a beach, a car dump, an airport, a church,* or *a market*. Other suggestions for focuses: *draw and describe your hand; close up photos of insects; trees and flowers; candle flames; thunder and lightning; faces; animals, insects, birds, fish.*

As a group, brainstorm words and ideas about the subject. Jot down the main things you can see down the centre of the board, e.g. looking at a bull might generate: *horns, eyes, tail*. Then flesh out each idea: *Tasselled tail swishes*. Add a 'what does it look like' column for similes. Generate the similes by asking 'what does it remind you of?': *Tasselled tail swishes like a bell pull.*

Then encourage the children to use the list of ideas to craft a simple, descriptive free verse poem about the subject, reminding them to add powerful language and use a dash of poetic technique.

Using the Poems

Listen carefully to how the actor performs the poems. Use their performances as models for children in groups to perform chorally.

The Magnificent Bull (p 15)

This poem introduces the idea of writing a 'praise poem' – in praise of a special creature. The writer uses similes to describe the bull. You could follow the reading and discussion by generating similes to describe a different creature – it is helpful to have a picture.

- Listen to the actor reading the poem and discuss first impressions.
- Read through line by line, discussing and interpreting.
- How do you know that this was written in another country?
- Discuss any difficult words, e.g. *Hornbill.*
- Who wrote this and what do they feel about the bull?
- Which words or images are most powerful?
- Look at similes – create other similes, e.g. what would the bull's horns look like?
- Draw a bull and label the picture with similes from the poem.

The Locust (p 17)

This is another poem from a distant country and another culture. However, the locust is not to be praised because it brings desolation. Explain how farmers fear locusts. The poem moves on from similes, introducing metaphor.

- Listen to, read and discuss.
- Who wrote this and what do they feel about the locust?
- Notice how nearly all of the images are written as metaphors. Tease out the difference between the metaphor and the simile.
- Draw attention to the opening question, 'What is a locust?' This could be a useful opening for the children's own writing about a creature.
- Watch the section in the programme where the children are looking at the locusts and use these images to brainstorm new similes. Remind the children how to turn the similes into metaphors.
- Draw and label the locust using images from the poem or new images.
- For writing, use a close-up photo of an insect (or other creature) and brainstorm descriptive words and similes that can be turned into metaphors.

Meet the Poet

Brian Patten's children's poetry collections are published by Puffin. He is one of Britain's foremost children's poets. Brian's poems range from the humorous to more serious inventions. He also writes stories for children. A passionate believer in the imagination, Brian's poetry is important for key stage 2 children to have enjoyed, performed and discussed.

- Listen to, read and discuss the poem he reads: *A Boat in the Snow* (p 16).
- Discuss how the poet feels about the experience.
- Which parts are the most powerful. What sort of picture does the poet create? How does the line make you feel?
- What does the poem remind you of?
- Look for examples of metaphors, e.g. *the ocean's cold dark skin.*
- Find the example of personification – *the white blizzard is swallowed.*
- Sketch the scene, looking for clues in the poem.
- Hot seat the character in the poem.
- Turn the poem into a diary entry.

PROGRAMME 2 – MEMORIES

Programme 2 focuses on the *original playfulness with language and ideas, detailed recreation of closely observed experience*, and *using different patterns* writing strands outlined in the primary strategy 'poetry progression'. The programme is about using memory and/or experiences that have mattered or seem significant, and poems that capture a moment or important event. Writers such as Michael Rosen have used their memories to record significant everyday moments in their lives.

The challenge set in this programme is to: *write and perform a poem based on a memory or experience; prepare a polished poem to perform.*

You will need some sort of focus for writing in your classroom – this may well arise out of the memory searches and anecdote sessions in the following games.

Writing warm up games

The following games are intended to help children generate words and ideas, to recall memories, use details to recreate experiences, use powerful language, similes and metaphor.

Warming up the mind

To help the children begin to generate ideas and language without being self-critical, play the 'ink waster' game. Suggest a title, and then give the children a minute to write as much about it as they can. They do not have to know anything because they can make it up. Set it as a challenge – who can write the most in one minute? Do not worry about what they write – the exercise is just to get them generating ideas rapidly without worrying.

Developing poetic technique

Using 'powerful' words Provide the children with sentences that are dull and use weak language. The children have to 'improve' the sentences. Try giving them 'boring' sentences to enliven.

Inventing similes ('like' or 'as') Provide some images for the children to use to generate similes.

Using metaphors experiment by turning the similes into metaphors.

Using sound effects Play a quick-fire alliterative game – say a type of animal and ask the children to come up with alliterative phrases or sentences.

Using the Programme

Memory search

Play several quick games that rely on memory searches. Make lists of *sad times, funny times, memorable moments, times I was in trouble, great/terrible holidays, moving house, changing schools*, etc. Everyone should jot down a few ideas – it helps if you tell a few anecdotes first of all to trigger the children's thinking. Then put the class in pairs so that they can share anecdotes, based on their memories.

Memory poem

You could then try a few list poem ideas such as:

- 5 excuses for being late to school.
- When my friend left school, I remembered…
- What would you take to a desert island – favourite pet, friend, item, memory?

- Two-minute 'ink waster' – choose a memory and write about it as fast as you can without stopping. It could be something quite small like taking the dog for a walk.
- Confession – splurge write a list of confessions – naughty things you did that no one ever found out about when you were younger.
- Scabs – everyone has a scab, or has had one. How did it happen? Splurge write.
- List 'things I would like to do but cannot'.

Model ideas so that the children have some examples that they can follow. All these snippets of ideas and writing can be stored away for later embellishment. Part of the secret will be alighting upon an experience that seems worth writing about. It doesn't have to be something impressively dramatic – indeed, the best may well be the everyday carefully observed/recalled experiences.

Memories of the House

Are there any interesting buildings near the school? If so, either visit or take photos.

Discuss with the children how places might have memories – what might this building have seen or overheard? Use the idea of the building as a silent witness to its past. Supposing it was given a voice? What memories might it talk about? Children could be in role as different rooms – what did they hear or see?

- Invent or discover names of previous inhabitants or pets.
- Use simple frameworks for imaginary writing: *This room once heard/saw…, This house has seen/heard…, If these walls could speak they would tell you about…, Long ago I heard/saw…, This room recalls…,* e.g.

This room once heard
The steady snore of an evacuee,
And the latenight sobs
As he hurt for his Mother
And dreamed of his Father.

Memories of images or objects

In the programme the children create a group poem about a souvenir elephant, imagining what it might be remembering and thinking. Use the same sort of idea in your class. Each child selects or is given an object or image, e.g. *stone, door, window, tree, ring, clock,* **etc. The children are timed and have two or three minutes to write down what the object remembers. Get them to write in role as 'I', pretending that they are the object speaking. For example:**

The stone's first memory – I remember waiting patiently at the roadside till the Sunday school mistress kicked me into the stream.

The clock's first memory – As my first tick tocked, I remember watching two girls playing with their yoyos and the strings becoming entangled – like their lives.

The ring's most painful memory – I was tugged from my lady's finger and thrown into the road as she stamped her foot. I lay there, cold and silent, waiting for sunlight to turn me into a miniature halo.

Using the Memory Boxes

Ask each child to create a memory box – this could be a real box with photos, objects and so on, or a drawing of a memory box (label items that might be inside it). Get them to show what they have brought or drawn and to tell the memory that goes with different items.

This could lead into discussing or the children deciding which item might be worth using as a trigger for a poem.

Demonstrate how to write a simple free verse poem based on a memory, e.g.

When I was eight,
I got lost at the zoo –
I remember stumbling
Like a drunkard
Amongst adults
Vast as sailing ships
Whilst I was the little dinghy adrift
In an uncharted sea…

They may need to 'tell the experience' onto the page rather like an anecdote, and then shave it back, using some technique to hone its poignancy. It can help to get them to read their writing aloud and to listen for the parts that flow like free verse and which bits descend into prose-like storytelling.

Other ideas

Explain how the children can use a repeating pattern to write about memories, e.g. *I remember seeing… I remember tasting… I remember hearing…*

Listen to Jackie Kay's poem *Red Running Shoes*, **discuss the poem and then use it as a basis for the children to write about their own memories, either in prose or poem form.**

Using The Poems

Bits of Early Days (p 20)

- Discuss likes, dislikes, puzzles and pattern.
- Look for specific details that bring the poem alive by giving localised rather than generalised information. Discuss the need for this in their own writing.
- Use the poem as a model for their own memory poem using the same pattern – what parts of their earliest days would they recall?

Fishbones Dreaming (p 22)

- Talk the poem through line by line and discuss.
- Why did the poet write this do you think?
- What other sorts of strange objects might hold dreams or secrets?

Meet the Poet

Michael Rosen is probably the best-known and most popular poet writing for children at the moment. Many of his poems are about his own childhood and about his own children when they were growing up. He has an anecdotal style that lends itself well to reading aloud. But don't be fooled by the appearance of simplicity – the poems are sparse, exact and reflect universal truths about family life and relationships. He is also a fantastic performer.

- Read more poems by Michael Rosen.
- Perform the poems alone or in pairs, and record the performances.
- Make a video for other classes – a poetry programme.
- Hot seat the main character from the poem Chocolate Cake.
- Hot seat his Mum after the event.
- Listen again to the interview and note the short poem *Down behind a dustbin, I met a dog called Jim*. Use this as a basis for writing other silly rhyming poems, using the same formula.

PROGRAMME 3 – IMAGINARY WORLDS

Programme 3 focuses on the *original playfulness with language and ideas* strand outlined in the primary strategy 'poetry progression'. The programme is about experimenting playfully with language and ideas in a surreal manner to create new combinations and surprises. It covers word play and nonsense verse as well as the creation of surreal ideas.

The challenge set in this programme is to: *write and perform an imaginative poem; using words in interesting and playful combinations; to surprise the reader.*

You will need some sort of focus for writing in your classroom – this may well be the model poems in the programme or one of the ideas listed below.

Writing warm up games

These games are intended to help children generate words and ideas, to observe closely, use powerful language, similes and metaphor.

Warming up the mind

Play the 'ink waster' game (see notes for programme 2) just to get the children generating words and ideas rapidly – a sort of linguistic mental gymnastics. This is handy for loosening up the mind.

Creating new combinations

Write up a sentence such as *The tired soldier ran through the deep forest.* Then ask the children to change the adjectives so that they are impossible. One way to do this is to suggest that they start with the same letter, e.g. *The tasty soldier ran through the donut forest.* This is harder than it seems – dictionaries can be used.

Push the children to try out new and unexpected combinations. This could be done by making a list of 'things' (nouns), starting with a chosen letter, e.g. *parrot, pliers, paint porpoise.* Hide this list and then make a list of random adjectives starting with a different letter, e.g. *trembling, tiny, terrific, tatty.* Dictionaries can help this activity – the secret though is to keep the lists separate. Once you have done both lists, bring them together: *a trembling parrot, a tiny pair of pliers, terrific paint, a tatty porpoise.* You could create combinations using initials – get everyone to make a list of crazy combinations using their own initials. This can be done by working in pairs. One child generates the noun while the other generates the adjectives and then hands them over.

Creating new ideas

In the programme the children are asked to play the 'what if?' game. Watch this and then play the game in class. Begin by listing on a board all sorts of possible topics – *things in the room, things you can see from the window, things in the country, things in the town, things at home, animals,* etc. then let the children loose to invent some 'what ifs'.

Developing poetic technique

You will need to play a few simple games at various points to develop poetic technique:

Inventing similes ('like' or 'as') Invent mad similes that do not make any sense at all by writing any old thing down or writing something impossible or daft. Start with similes based on *as … as,* e.g. *As thin as a hippo.* Now move into crazy similes using *like* in which you just invent any old thing – the odder the better! E.g. *The moon is like a zebra in hot pants.*

Using metaphors Try playing the 'furniture game' just to loosen up the mind and tune into metaphorical thinking. Everyone writes down 'he is...', 'she is...', 'you are...' or 'I am...'.

Explain that anything goes, and offer ideas – *You are a lazy lizard languishing, I am a bud exploding in May* – to get them started. Suggest various categories – *animal, nature, tiny object, character from a book, piece of furniture, colour, emotion,* etc.

Using personification Make a list of objects and use personification to turn them into a wacky Disney world, e.g. *In my Disney World, the chairs tiptoe home, the clock wolf whistles at the moon, the books sprout wings and fly, the tables crack jokes and the doors creak their knees like old men.*

Using sound effects Play a quick-fire alliterative game – this could begin with you saying an animal and the children thinking of alliterative phrases or sentences, and move on to writing sentences that alliterate but purposefully choose words that do not usually go together: *The designer dog detonated a ditch of dreary dandruff.*

Nonsense words Make a list of two-syllable words on a board (e.g. *cowboy, running, drumbeat, Sunday*), then separate the words into their separate syllables: *cow – boy, runn – ing, drum – beat, Sun – day.* Now shuffle the front and end bits around to create a set of new words: *cowing, Sunboy, drumday, runbeat.*

Ask the children to invent new words in this way. When they all have three new words, they swap with a partner who then has to write a few sentences using the new words, e.g. *The sunboy was cowing down the lake. It was Drumday and the runbeat was about to begin.*

Collect good examples Get the children to scan through poetry collections, looking for unusual combinations, wild similes and nonsense words.

Using the Programme

Poetry Treasure Trail

Use the poems in this programme as models for writing. Magical boxes and secret doors are especially good starting points. It is worth having a 'writing box' in the classroom. Over a period of time gather in your box images, postcards, photos, cuttings, cards, objects that might be useful for writing – anything unusual, curious or bizarre. Each child selects an object or photo of something from the box or brings something from home in a box of their own. Or take the children on a walk round the school. They should note anything of interest or use a digital camera to photograph things. These items can then be used as starting points for a class poem or individual poems. Tease out the underlying pattern: *I found it… It is made of… If let loose, it can… It dreams of… If you saw it, you would…*

Secrets poem

Children respond well to creating secrets. I often begin this session by asking the children about secrets – though you may warn them to be cautious about sharing a 'real' secret. A fun idea is to begin inventing secrets that objects might have. For instance, what sort of secrets could a stone tell? *a sparrow stole a crumb, the wind is trying to blow the leaves away, I have a spark trapped inside of me.*

Hand out small strips of paper and everyone has to write a magical secret – an invented idea – onto the paper. For example, a magical secret about the moon: *When it is daytime, the moon sleeps.* Put these into a hat and everyone picks out a secret to read out.

Move onto something more adventurous by creating a class secret and brainstorm a range of ideas for a poem, using the model *My secret is made of… I found it… This secret can… If I lost it….* They may not wish to make a secret – what else could be made? *a promise, a wish, a dream, a nightmare, a hope, a laugh, a scream*?

Using The Poems

Listen carefully to how the actor performs the poems. Use their performances as models for children in groups to perform chorally.

Jabberwocky (p 29)

- Discuss likes, dislikes, puzzles and pattern.
- Best words and ideas?
- Discuss word meanings.
- Play a game inventing new words and putting them into sentences.
- Write definitions for the new words.
- Swap the new words into the poem and perform a new version with these words.

The Sound Collector (p 30)

- Likes dislikes, puzzles, pattern.
- What is the most powerful/memorable idea?
- Play the blindfold game from the programme and write extra ideas, following the same pattern.
- What would a taste collector collect, or a sight or touch collector?

The Door (p 32)

- Discuss likes, dislikes, puzzles and pattern.
- What are the most powerful words and ideas?
- Pick through it line by line, discussing meanings – what does it make you see or feel or think about?
- Look at how the author creates atmosphere or surprises the reader.
- Miroslav Holub's poem makes a great model for writing something imaginary. It can help to invent different sorts of doors. The simplest idea is to have different colours – what might be found through the scarlet door? To begin, make a list of scarlet things, e.g.

Through the scarlet door
I found a sunset crying for the darkness,
A letter box closing its mouth,
A heart waiting for its rib cage,
A traffic light's warning…

You could make the doors more interesting by having them associated with more intriguing concepts, e.g.

Thought the door of anger
I found your cruel words stapled together.

Through the door of sorrow
I found all the goodbyes ever spoken…

Instead of doors you could suggest magical windows or a magical gate or tunnel.

Meet the Poet

Kit Wright's children's poetry collections make perfect reading for key stage 2 classes. His poems can be humorous or serious, and are always beautifully crafted and elegant. *The Magic Box* **is a great tool to stimulate writing. It never fails to release imaginative ideas.**

- Listen to, read and discuss the poem *The Magic Box* (p 31)
- How do the ideas change through the poem?
- What sorts of techniques and tricks is Kit using?

PROGRAMME 4 – RHYTHM AND RHYME

Programme 4 focuses on the *performance* and *using different patterns* strands outlined in the primary strategy 'poetry progression'. The programme is about writing a poem that uses rhythm and rhyme as its dominant feature, with the words producing a beat and impact, as much as the meaning. Raps, rants and songs would be the nearest equivalent.

The challenge set in this programme is to: *write and perform a polished performance poem; using rhythm or rhyme; avoiding using rhymes that don't make sense.*

You will need some sort of focus for writing in your classroom – this may well be the model poems in the programme or one of the ideas listed below.

Writing warm up games

These games are intended to help children generate words and ideas, use details to recreate experiences, use powerful language, similes and metaphor as well as writing with rhythm and some use of rhyme without destroying meaning.

Warming up the mind

Start with some word association, or the 'ink waster' game (see notes for programme 2) – just to get the children generating words and ideas rapidly – a sort of linguistic mental gymnastics. This is handy for loosening up the mind.

Developing poetic technique

You will need to play a few simple games at various points to develop poetic technique:

Using 'powerful' words Provide the children with sentences that are dull and use weak language. The children have to 'improve' the sentences. Try giving them 'boring'; sentences to enliven.

Inventing similes ('like' or 'as') Provide some images for the children to use to generate similes.

Using metaphors experiment by turning the similes into metaphors.

Using sound effects Play a quick-fire alliterative game – this could with you saying an animal and the children thinking of alliterative phrases or sentences.

Tuning in to rhythm and rhyme

- Say your name and clap the beat.
- Pass the beat around the group.
- Change the beat and pass it on.
- Take a word and generate rhymes. These work well: *train, wheel, bone, light, flies, soap, seed, snail, goat, cream, face, five, bowl, cake, hook, car, sock, back, shout, wood, led, bad, toy, day, gate, see, try, blow, true, game, gave, fine, moon, fool, boast, feet, cap, ash, rat, day, best, ill, bit, line, ring, ink, ship, shot, stop, hump, poke, mug.*

Rhyming places It can be fun to generate rhyming snapshots by using place names. Make a list, then invent simple rhymes, e.g. *In Stroud I was loud.*

Rhyming names Try writing short poems using invented names, e.g.

Colin Short
Liked playing sport

Andy Dill
Felt very ill

Choruses Make a list of favourite words and then invent silly choruses, e.g.

Avocado, avocado
Green and shiny
As a fist.
Avocado, avocado
When you're gone
You will be missed!

Don't worry too much about sense. Have fun playing with rhythms and rhymes – remember too that you can say something rhythmically that does not rhyme.

Rhyming dreams Try an activity where you base a rhyming poem on a simple frame, e.g. *You make me dream of…*

You make me dream of a garden gnome.
You make me dream of the wrong way home.

You make me dream of Tony Blair.
You make me dream of having no hair…

Using the Programme

At the Farm

In the programme you can see the children using sounds and words to create rhythms. Get the children collecting and making a note of things they see and hear. These lists can be used in a class poem. You could look for 'found' sounds, sights and words. 'Found' words are ones that you find lying around – on boards, notices, scraps of paper. Try a two word rhyming pattern with the words, e.g.

Sheep bleating, lambs competing.
Tractors churning, sheep dog yearning.

Try using some of the found words, e.g.

No entry, No entry –
They're trying to keep us out.

Without
No entry, No entry
we'd be in without a doubt.

Ghostly Poem

Play Paul Cookson's poem *We Are Not Alone* several times. The class could imitate his rhythm and try a choral performance. Make a list of ghostly sounds that you might hear at night and things that you might see. Then use a simple frame to create a rhyming poem, e.g.

Late at night –

when the floorboards quiver
and nightmares speak,

when the taps drop drips
and the doorways creak,

when the windows rattle
and the trees all shake,

when the shadows shiver
and the moon's awake…

Try performing in hushed voices to create a ghostly effect and include some background sounds to add impact.

Other ideas

- Listen to Kit Wright's *Zoe's Earrings*. Try writing more verses.
- Use nursery rhymes as a basis for new poems – change some of the words to create a new rhyme.
- Write out the words to any popular pop song. Change words to create a new version.

Using The Poems

The Dragon Who Ate Our School (p 35)

- Perform the poem as a group. Experiment by using different voices for different parts and add in simple percussion and sound effects, e.g. claps.
- Illustrate different parts of the poem.
- Video a performance and insert the illustrations into the video to create a multi-media performance.

The Visitor (p 37)

- Hot seat the characters.
- Re-tell the story as a diary, letter or phone call to a friend.
- What is the skeleton's story?
- How does the poet use techniques to make it scary?
- Perform the poem in groups – use simple sound effects or chime bars to add impact.

We Are Not Alone (p 39)

- Discuss Paul's performance – what makes it effective?
- Try performing the poem – this helps the children to internalise the rhythm and should be done before they write a version themselves.

Meet the Poet

Valerie Bloom is one of the country's best performance poets for children. Her poems reflect her varied background, from her upbringing in the Caribbean to her life in England. She started writing poetry at an early age and writes for both adults and children both in patois and standard English.

- Listen, discuss and then perform along with the video of Val performing *Pinda Cake.*
- Note Val's points about poetry: *you must read it aloud because poetry is 'word of mouth'; train your senses; a poet sees things in more detail; a poet hears more sharply.*
- Listen to and discuss the extra poem *Who's Dem Boots.*
- Try performing the poem. The feet marching need to act as an ominous background to the verses – and make sure the ending is a dramatic cut off.
- Discuss what the ending signifies.
- Explain to the children the background of the poem – Val explains various references to conflicts where different groups have been severely oppressed.

PCM 1

The Magnificent Bull
Traditional – Dinka Tribe

My bull is white like the silver fish in the river,
White like the shimmering crane bird on the river bank,
White like fresh milk!
His roar is like the thunder to the Turkish cannon on the
Steep shore.
My bull is dark like the rain cloud in the storm
He is like summer and winter.
Half of him is dark like the storm cloud,
Half of him is light like sunshine.
His back shines like the morning star.
His brow is red like the beak of the Hornbill.
His forehead is like a flag, calling the people from a distance;
He resembles the rainbow.

I will water him at the river,
With my spear I shall drive me enemies.
Let them water their herds at the well;
The river belongs to me and my bull.
Drink my bull, from the river; I am here
To guard you with my spear.

PCM 2

A Boat in the Snow
Brian Patten

On to the ocean's cold dark skin
Snowflakes are falling and are melting away
How strange the snow seems out here
How quickly the blizzard is
Swallowed up by the waves
Without a framework of land
Each flake is transformed into a million
Ocean born moths
They flicker into existence
Then go
As the sky above me and around me
Glitters with frosty flecks of stars
So the deck of the boat glitters
And I wonder
Are whales sleeping out there
In the ocean's depths
And I wonder
Do whales really sleep and how
There's no-one to ask
Snuggled up in their cabins
The crew were dreaming and all around
Me still the snow is falling
And the ship's deck has become a moonlit field
A field adrift on the dark skin of the wild
I would love to sail for ever
Between islands of snow.

PCM 3

The Locust
Traditional Madagascan poem
(Translated by A.Marre and Willard. R Trask)

What is a locust?
Its head, a grain of corn; its neck, the hinge of a knife;
Its horns, a bit of thread; its chest is smooth and burnished;
Its body is like a knife-handle;
Its hock, a saw; its spittle, ink;
Its underwings, clothing for the dead.
On the ground – it is laying eggs;
In flight – it is like the clouds.
Approaching the ground, it is rain glittering in the sun;
Lighting on a plant, it becomes a pair of scissors;
Walking, it becomes a razor;
Desolation walks with it.

PCM 4

The Oldest Girl In The World
Carol Ann Duffy

Children, I remember how I could hear
With my soft young ears
The tiny sounds of the air –
Tinkles and chimes
Like minuscule bells
Ringing continually there
Clinks and chinks
Like glasses of sparky gooseberry wine,
Jolly and glinting and raised in the air
Yes, I could hear like a bat. And how!
Can't hear a sniff of it now.

Truly, believe me, I could all the time see
Every insect that crawled in a bush,
Every bird that hid in a tree,
Individually.
If I wanted to catch a caterpillar
To keep as a pet in a box
I had only to watch a cabbage
And there it would be,
Crawling bendy and green towards me.
Yes, I could see with the eyes of a cat. Miaow!
Can't see a sniff of it now.

And my sense of taste was second to none.
By God, the amount I knew with my tongue!
The shrewd taste of a walnut's brain.
The taste of a train from a bridge.
Of a kiss. Of air chewy with midge.
Of fudge from a factory two miles away
From the house where I lived.
I'd stick out my tongue
To savour the sky in a droplet of rain.
Yes, I could taste like the fang of a snake! Wow!
Can't taste a sniff of it now.

On the scent, what couldn't I smell
With my delicate nose, my nostrils of pearl?
I could smell the world!
Snow. Soot. Soil.
Satsumas in their Christmas sock.
The ink of a pen
The stink of an elephant's skin.
The blue broth of a swimming pool. Dive in!
The showbizzy gasp of the wind.
Yes, I could smell like a copper's dog. Bow-wow!
Can't smell a sniff of it now.

As for my sense of touch
It was too much!
The cold of a snowball
felt through the vanishing heat of a mitt.
A peach like an apple wearing a vest.
The raffia dish of a bird's nest
A hot chestnut
Branding the palm at the heart of the fist
The stab of the thorn on the rose. Long grass, its itch.
Yes, I could feel with the sensitive hand of a ghost.
Whoooo!
Can't feel a sniff of it now

Can't see a
Can't hear a
Can't taste a
Can't smell a
Can't feel a bit of it whiff of it niff of it
Can't get a sniff of it now.

PCM 5

Bits of Early Days
James Berry

Still a shock to remember
facing that attacking
dog's fangs and eyes at its gate.
Seeing our slug-eating dog come in
the house, mouth gummed up, plastered.

Still a joy to remember
standing at our palm-fringed beach
watching the sunrise streak the sea.
Finding a hen's nest in high grass
full of eggs.
Galloping a horse barebacked
over the village pasture.

Still a shock to remember
eating with fingers and caught
oily handed by my teacher.
Seeing a dog like a goat-hide flattened
There in the road.

Still a joy to remember
myself a small boy milking a cow
in new sunlight.
Smelling asafoetida on
a village baby I held.
Sucking fresh honey from its comb
just robbed.

Still a shock to remember
watching weighted kittens tossed in
the sea's white breakers.
Seeing our village stream dried up
with rocks exposed
like dry guts and brains.

Still a joy to remember
walking barefoot on a bed of dry leaves
there in deep woods.
Finding my goat with all of three
new wobbly kids.

Still a shock to remember
facing that youth-gang attack and all
the needless abuse.
Holding my first identity card
stamped 'Negro'.

Still a joy to remember
walking fourteen miles from four a.m.
into town market.
Surrounded by sounds of church-bell
in sunlight and birdsong.

PCM 6

Fishbones Dreaming
Matthew Sweeney

Fishbones lay in the smelly bin.
He was a head, a backbone and a tail.
Soon the cats would be in for him.

He didn't like to be this way.
He shut his eyes and dreamed back.

Back to when he was fat, and hot on a plate
Beside green beans, with lemon juice
squeezed on him. And a man with a knife
And fork raised, about to eat him.

He didn't like to be this way.
He shut his eyes and dreamed back

Back to when he was frozen in the freezer.
With lam cutlets and minced beef and prawns.
Three months he was in there.

He didn't like to be this way.
He shut his eyes and dreamed back

Back to when he was squirming in a net,
With thousand of other fish, on the deck
Of a boat. And the rain falling
Wasn't wet enough to breathe in.

He didn't like to be this way.
He shut his eyes and dreamed back

Back to when he was darting through the sea,
past crabs and jellyfish, and others
Like himself. Or surfacing to jump for flies
And feel the sun on his face.

He liked to be this way.
He dreamed hard to try and stay there.

PCM 7

Chocolate Cake
Michael Rosen

I love chocolate cake.
And when I was a boy
I loved it even more.

Sometimes we used to have it for tea
and Mum used to say,
"If there's any left over
you can take it to school
tomorrow to have at playtime.'
And the next day I would take it to school
wrapped up in tin foil
open it up at playtime and sit in the
corner of the playground
eating it,
you know how the icing on top
is all shiny and it cracks as you
bite into it
and there's that other kind of icing in
the middle
and it sticks to your hands and you
can lick your fingers
and lick your lips
oh it's lovely.
yeah.

Anyway,
once we had this chocolate cake for tea
and later I went to bed
but while I was in bed
I found myself waking up
licking my lips
and smiling.
I woke up proper.
'The chocolate cake.'
It was the first thing
I thought of.

I could almost see it
so I thought,
what if I go downstairs
and have a little nibble, yeah?

It was all dark
everyone was in bed
so it must have been really late
but I got out of bed,
crept out of the door

there's always a creaky floorboard, isn't there?

Past Mum and Dad's room,

careful not to tread on bits of broken toys
or bits of Lego
you know what it's like treading on Lego
with your bare feet,

yowwwwww
shhhhhhh

downstairs
into the kitchen
open the cupboard
and there it is
all shining.

So I take it out of the cupboard
put it on the table
and I see that
there's a few crumbs lying about on the plate,
so I lick my finger and run my finger all over the
crumbs
scooping them up
and put them into my mouth

Oooooooooommmmm-mmmm
nice.

Then
I look again
and on one side where it's been cut,
it's all crumbly.
So I take a knife
I think I'll just tidy that up a bit,
cut off the crumbly bits
scoop them all up
and into the mouth

oooommmmm mmmmm

nice.

Look at the cake again.

That looks a bit funny now,
one side doesn't match the other
I'll just even it up a bit, eh?

Take the knife
and slice.
This time the knife makes a little cracky noise
as it goes through that hard icing on top.

A whole slice this time,

into the mouth.

Oh the icing on top
and the icing in the middle
ohhhhhh ooooo mmmmmmm

But now
I cant stop myself.
Knife –
I just take any old slice at it
and I've got this great big chunk
and I'm cramming it in
what a greedy pig
but it's so nice,

and there's another
and another and I'm squealing and I'm smacking my lips

and I'm stuffing myself with it
and
before I know,
I've eaten the lot.
The whole lot.
I look at the plate.
It's all gone.

Oh no
they're bound to notice, aren't they,
a whole chocolate cake doesn't just disappear
does it?

What shall I do?

I know. I'll wash the plate up,
and the knife

and put them away and maybe no one
will notice, eh?

So I do that
and creep creep creep
back to bed
into bed
doze off
licking my lips
with a lovely feeling in my belly.
Mmmmmmmm

In the morning I get up,
downstairs,
have breakfast,
Mum's saying
'Have you got your dinner money?'
and I say,
"yes."
'And don't forget to take some chocolate cake with you.'
I stopped breathing.

'What's the matter,' she says,
'you normally jump at chocolate cake?'

I'm still not breathing,
and she's looking at me very closely now.

She's looking at me just below my mouth.
'Whats that? She says.
'Whats what?' I say.
'It looks like chocolate,' she says.
'Its not chocolate cake is it?'
No answer.
'Is it?'
'I don't know.'
She goes to the cupboard
looks in, up, top, middle, bottom,
turns back to me.
'It's gone.
It's gone.
You haven't eaten it, have you?'
'I don't know.'
'You don't know? You don't know if you've eaten a
whole
chocolate cake or not?
When? When did you eat it?

So I told her,

and she said
well what could she say?
'That's the last time I give you any cake to take
to school.
Now go. Get out
no wait
not before you've washed your dirty sticky face.'
I went upstairs
looked in the mirror
and there it was,
just below my mouth,
a chocolate smudge.
The give-away.
Maybe she'll forget about it by next week.

PCM 8

Red Running Shoes
Jackie Kay

I wore some other girl's red running shoes
with real spikes like rose thorns under my foot.

I got into position: my limbs seriously tense,
one knee on the asphalt, one foot flat, all that.

I crouched over, hands down, like a predator
ready for prey; and took off, took flight

on the red running track, so fast I could be fear
running, a live fright, a chance vision.

My dark hair wild in the wind.
My arms pounding light years, thin air, euphoria.

I flew past in some other girl's red running shoes
round the red track, near the railway line.

I raced straight towards the future.
The past left standing behind, waving.

I ran and ran; my feet became the land.
I couldn't tell if the ground was moving under my feet

shifting sand, or if I might ever just stop like a heartbeat.
It felt as if I could run for ever, hard pounding feet

Until I ran into myself, years on
sat still, heavy, pasty forty, groaning the streak lightning gone.

Jabberwocky
Lewis Carroll

(from Through the Looking-Glass and What Alice Found There, 1872)

`Twas brillig, and the slithy toves
Did gyre and gimble in the wabe:
All mimsy were the borogoves,
And the mome raths outgrabe.

"Beware the Jabberwock, my son!
The jaws that bite, the claws that catch!
Beware the Jubjub bird, and shun
The frumious Bandersnatch!"

He took his vorpal sword in hand:
Long time the manxome foe he sought —
So rested he by the Tumtum tree,
And stood awhile in thought.

And, as in uffish thought he stood,
The Jabberwock, with eyes of flame,
Came whiffling through the tulgey wood,
And burbled as it came!

One, two! One, two! And through and through
The vorpal blade went snicker-snack!
He left it dead, and with its head
He went galumphing back.

"And, has thou slain the Jabberwock?
Come to my arms, my beamish boy!
O frabjous day! Callooh! Callay!'
He chortled in his joy.

`Twas brillig, and the slithy toves
Did gyre and gimble in the wabe;
All mimsy were the borogoves,
And the mome raths outgrabe.

PCM 10

The Sound Collector
Roger Mcgough

A stranger called this morning
Dressed all in black and grey
Put every sound into a bag
And carried it away

The whistling of the kettle
The turning of the lock
The purring of the kitten
The ticking of the clock

The popping of the toaster
The crunching of the flakes
When you spread the marmalade
The scraping noise it makes

The hissing of the frying pan
The ticking of the grill
The bubbling of the bath tub
As it starts to fill

The drumming of the raindrops
On the window pane
When you do the washing up
The gurgle of the drain

The crying of the baby
The squeaking of the chair
The swishing of the curtain
The creaking of the stair

A stranger called this morning
He didn't leave his name
Left us only silence
Life will never be the same.

PCM 11

The Magic Box
Kit Wright

I will put in the box

The swish of a silk sari on a summer night,
Fire from the nostrils of a Chinese dragon,
The top of a tongue touching a tooth.

I will put in the box

A snowman with a rumbling belly,
A sip of the bluest water from Lake Lucerne,
A leaping spark from an electric fish.

I will put in the box

Three violet wishes spoken in Gujarati,
The last joke of an ancient uncle
And the first smile of a baby.

I will put in the box

A fifth season and a black sun,
A cowboy on a broomstick
And a witch on a white horse.

My box is fashioned from ice and gold and steel,
With stars on the lid and secrets in the corners.
Its hinges are the toe joints
Of dinosaurs.

I shall surf on my box
On the great high-rolling breaks of the wild Atlantic,
Then wash ashore on a yellow beach
The colour of the sun.

PCM 12

The Door
Miroslav Holub

Go and open the door
Maybe outside there's
A tree, or a wood,
A garden,
Or a magic city

Go and open the door.
Maybe a dog's rummaging
Maybe you'll see a face,
Or an eye, or the picture
Of a picture

Go and open the door.
If there's a fog
It will clear.

Go and open the door.
Even if there's only
The darkness ticking,
Even if there's only
The hollow wind,
Even if
Nothing
Is there,
Go and open the door.

At least
There'll be a draught.

PCM 13

Zoe's Ear-rings
Kit Wright

She bought 'em in the autumn
After spotting 'em in Nottingham.
She took 'em home to Cookham
And she put 'em in a drawer

Till May came the the day came
When she wore 'em down to Shoreham,
But nobody was for 'em
So she wore 'em nevermore...

Till the wedding of her sister
To a mister out at Bicester,
Name of Jimmy, who said, 'Gimme,'
So without 'em she went home,

But she nipped back down to nick 'em
For a knees-up in High Wycombe,
For an evening quite near Chevening
And a dawn at Kilmacolm.

They were in 'er for a dinner
Which was excellent, in Pinner,
And another one, a cracker,
In Majacca - that's in Spain -

Then she popped 'em on in Haddenham
And didn't feel too bad in 'em:
She felt in 'em, in Cheltenham,
Just as right as rain.

They looked smart on in Dumbarton,
They looked wizard on the Lizard,
They looked corking down in Dorking
And incredible in Crewe.

When she wore 'em in Rugely
They impressed the people hugely,
While in Fordham folk adored 'em,
And they loved 'em in West Looe!

The citizens of Kettering
Had never seen a better ring,
In fact no better pair of 'em -
'Take care of 'em!' they cried.

Then she slithered into Lythham with 'em,
Shaking out a rhythm with 'em,
Wobb-er-ling and jogg-er-ling
Her head from side to side.

Folk in Preston thought the best 'un
Was the right 'un. In New Brighton
And in Sefton, though, the left 'un
Was the one they favoured more,

While in Greenham, when they'd seen 'em,
They said, 'How to choose between 'em?
What one praises in its brother,
In the other one is for!'

Then she tried 'em with new make-up
On a sponsored run round Bacup,
And at Norwich for a porridge-
Eating contest which she won,

But, spilling 'em in Gillingham,
Her lobes felt light in Willingham,
And nothing else is filling 'em,
So now

The poem's

Done!

PCM 14

The Dragon Who Ate Our School
Nick Tozcek

The day the dragon came to call,
She ate the gate, the playground wall
And, slate by slate, the roof and all,
The staffroom, gym, and entrance hall
And every classroom, big or small.

So...
She's undeniably great.
She's absolutely cool,
The dragon who ate
The dragon who ate
The dragon who ate our school.

Pupils panicked. Teachers ran.
She flew at them with wide wingspan.
She slew a few and then began
To chew through the lollipop man,
Two parked cars and a Transit van.

Wow.
She's undeniably great.
She's absolutely cool,
The dragon who ate
The dragon who ate
The dragon who ate our school

She bit off the head of the head.
She said she was sad he was dead.
He bled and he bled and he bled.
And as she fed, her chin went red
And then she swallowed the cycle shed.

Oh
She's undeniably great.
She's absolutely cool,
The dragon who ate

The dragon who ate
The dragon who ate our school

It's thanks to her that we've been freed.
We needn't write. We needn't read.
Me and my mates are all agreed,
We're very pleased with her indeed.
So clear the way, let her proceed.

Cos…
She's undeniably great.
She's absolutely cool,
The dragon who ate
The dragon who ate
The dragon who ate our school

There was some stuff she couldn't eat.
A monster forced to face defeat,
She pat it out along the street –
The dinner ladies' veg and meat
And that pink muck they serve for sweet.

But….
She's undeniably great.
She's absolutely cool,
The dragon who ate
The dragon who ate
The dragon who ate our school.

PCM 15

The Visitor
Ian Serraillier

A crumbling churchyard, the sea and the moon;
The waves had gouged out grave and bone;
A man was walking, late and alone.....

He saw a skeleton white on the ground;
A ring on a bony finger he found.

He ran home to his wife and gave her the ring.
Oh, where did you get it? He said not a thing.

'It's the loveliest ring in the world,' she said,
As it glowed on her finger. They slipped off to bed.

At midnight they woke. In the dark outside,
'Give me my ring!' a chill voice cried.

'What was that, William? What did it say?'
'Don't worry my dear. It'll soon go away'

'I'm coming!' A skeleton opened the door.
'Give me my ring!' it was crossing the floor

What was that, William? What did it say?
Don't worry my dear. It'll soon go away

I'm reaching you now! I'm climbing the bed.'
The wife pulled the sheet right over her head.

It was torn from her grasp and tossed in the air:
'I'll drag you out of your bed by the hair!'

'What was that William? What did it say?'
'Throw the ring through the window! THROW IT AWAY!'
She threw it. The skeleton leapt from the sill,
Scooped up the ring and clattered downhill,
Fainter......and fainter......Then all was still.

PCM 16

Pinda Cake
Valerie Bloom

De pinda cake lady comin'down
With her basket an' glass case she comin'to town,
She stop by de school gate an' set up her stall,
An while she a-set up, hear de ole lady bawl;

Pinda! Pinda cake!
Pinda! Pinda cake!
Gal an' bwoy me jus' done bake,
Come buy yuh lovely panda cake!

She have grater cake an she have duckunoo,
Coconut drops an' bulla cake too,
Kackass corn an' plantain tart,
But the t'ing dat dearest to me heart

Is Pinda! Pinda cake!
Pinda! Pinda cake!
Gal an' bwoy me jus' done bake,
Come buy yuh lovely pinda cake!

We all crowd round her an' yuh can tell
By de look o' de cake dem, an' de spicy smell
Dat they won't stay in de glass case fe too long,
As we buy from de lady, we join in de song.

Pinda! Pinda cake!
Pinda! Pinda cake!
Gal an' bwoy me jus' done bake,
Come buy yuh lovely pinda cake!

PCM 17

We Are Not Alone
Paul Cookson

When the floorboards creak and the hinges squeak
When the TV's off but seems to speak
When the moon is full and you hear a shriek
We are not alone.

When the spiders gather beneath your bed
When the colonise the garden shed
When they spin their webs right above your head
We are not alone.

When the lights are out and there's no one home
When you're by yourself and you're on your own
When the radiators bubble and groan
We are not alone.

When the shadows lengthen round your wall
When you hear deep breathing in the hall
When you think there's no one there at all
We are not alone.

When the branches tap on your window pane
When the finger twigs scritch scratch again
When something's changed but it looks the same
We are not alone.

When the wallpaper is full of eyes
When the toys in the dark all change in size
When anything's a monster in disguise
We are not alone

You'd better watch out whatever you do
There's something out there looking at you
When you think you are on your own
We are not
We are not
We are not alone.

PCM 18

Whose Dem Boots
Valerie Bloom

Whose dem boots ah hearin', chile,
Whose dem boots ah hear?
Whose dem boots ah hearin', chile,
Whose dem boots ah hear?
Dem boots trampin' down de road
Dat fill me heart wid fear?

Gotta fin' me a hid'n place,
Whai! Whai!
Gotta fin' me a hid'n place.

Whose dem boots ah hearin', chile,
Comin' thru me gate?
Whose dem boots ah hearin', chile,
Comin' thru me gate?
Trampin' straight up to me door?
Tell dem please to wait.

Gotta fin' me a hid'n place,
Whai! Whai!
Gotta fin' me a hid'n place.

Whose dem boots ah seein', chile,
Stand'n by me bed?
Whose dem boots ah seein', chile,
Stand'n by me bed?
Wait'n dere so patient, chile?
Tell dem go ahead.

Gotta fin' me a hid'n place,
Whai! Whai!
Gotta a fin' me a hid'n...Huh!